W9-AJR-694

Whose Tail Is This?

A Look at Tails—Swishing, Wiggling, and Rattling

Written by Peg Hall

Illustrated by Ken Landmark

Content Advisor: Julie Dunlap, Ph.D.

Reading Advisor: Lauren A. Liang, M.A.

Literacy Education, University of Minnesota

Minneapolis, Minnesota

PICTURE WINDOW BOOKS

Minneapolis, Minnesota

Editor: Lisa Morris Kee

Designer: Melissa Voda

Page production: The Design Lab

The illustrations in this book were prepared digitally.

Printed in the United States of America.

1 2 3 4 5 6 08 07 06 05 04 03

Library of Congress Cataloging-in-Publication Data

Hall, Peg.

  Whose tail is this? : a look at tails—swishing, wiggling, and rattling / written by Peg Hall; illustrated by Ken Landmark.

    p. cm. – (Whose is it?)

  Summary: Examines a variety of animal tails, noting how they look different and function in different ways.

  ISBN 1-4048-0011-5 (lib. bdg. : alk. paper)

  1. Tail—Juvenile literature. [1. Tail. 2. Animals.] I. Landmark, Ken, ill. II. Title.

  QL950.6 .H36 2003

  591.47–dc21   2002005774

Picture Window Books
5115 Excelsior Boulevard
Suite 232
Minneapolis, MN 55416
1-877-845-8392
www.picturewindowbooks.com

Here's a tale about who's who.

Look closely at an animal's tail. Tails can be long, short, or in-between. They can be hard and flat or soft and bendable. They can be furry, smooth, or full of feathers.

Some tails help animals keep their balance or swing from trees. Some tails make noise. Some tails fall off and grow back again.

Tails don't all look alike, because they don't all work alike.

Can you pin the tail on the right animal?

Look in the back for more fun facts about tails.

Whose tail is this, spread like a fan?

5

This is a peacock's tail.

Only the male peacock has such beautiful tail feathers.

Fun fact: A female peacock's tail feathers are shorter and duller than the male's. She does not want other animals to notice her when she is protecting her eggs.

A male peacock's tail is called a train.
He uses his tail to impress a female peacock.

Whose tail is this, holding on to a branch?

7

This is a spider monkey's tail.

The monkey uses its tail to hang from a branch. Now it can use both hands for eating.

Fun fact: Sometimes a baby spider monkey wraps its tail around its mother's legs or tail. The baby clings to its mother as she travels through the forest.

Whose tail is this, bouncing along?

This is a kangaroo's tail.

The tail sticks out behind the kangaroo.
That helps the kangaroo keep its
balance as it hops along.

Fun fact: A kangaroo
sometimes uses its tail like
another leg. When it fights,
the kangaroo leans back on
its tail and kicks its hind legs.

Whose tail is this, diving underwater?

11

This is a humpback whale's tail.

A whale's tail fins are called flukes.
The whale waves its flukes up and
down to swim very fast.

Fun fact: Humpback whales
talk to each other by slapping
their tails on the water. This is
called lobtailing. Lobtailing
also helps wash parasites off
the whale's tail.

Whose tail is this, waving back and forth?

This is a gecko lizard's tail.

The gecko waves its tail as an enemy comes close. When the enemy pounces on the tail, the tail breaks off.

The old tail keeps wiggling while the gecko runs away. Then the gecko grows a new tail.

Fun fact: It can take months for a gecko lizard to grow another tail. The new tail doesn't always look the same as the old one. It can be crooked or even a different color. Sometimes a gecko ends up with two or more tails at the same time.

14

Whose tail is this, making noise?

This is a rattlesnake's tail.

Hard rings of skin at the end of
the snake's long body make a
loud, rattling sound.

Fun fact: The
rattlesnake shakes
its tail so fast that
people see a blur
when the tail is
moving.

Rattlesnakes have a deadly bite.
When animals hear that rattle,
they know to stay away.

Whose tail is this, hanging on to seaweed?

This is a sea horse's tail.

The sea horse is a fish,
but it has a long, curled
tail like a monkey's.
When the sea horse is
resting, its tail holds on to
underwater plants. That
keeps the sea horse from
floating away.

Fun fact: Unlike other fish, the
sea horse swims with its head up
and its tail down. The tail helps the
sea horse balance as it swims.

Whose tail is this, pinned on tight?

This is your pretend tail!

You don't really have a tail. Do you wish you did? Would you use your tail to swing from treetops, or to push you through the ocean waves? Would your tail have feathers or rattles or fins? Would you like one tail or two?

Fun fact: Not all animals have tails. Apes don't have tails. Adult frogs don't have tails. There is even a cat with no tail called a Manx cat.

Just for Fun

Can you answer these riddles about tails?

My tail helps me keep my balance while I swim standing up. Who am I?

I am a sea horse.

My long tail can hold on to things just like your hand can. Who am I?

I am a spider monkey.

My tail makes a noise that tells other animals to stay away. Who am I?

I am a rattlesnake.

My wiggly tail can fall off when I'm attacked. Who am I?

I am a gecko.

My tail can spread out like a beautiful fan. Who am I?

I am a male peacock.

If you could have a tail, what would it look like? Draw yourself with your tail.

Fun Facts About Tails

BREAKAWAY TAILS When the gecko lizard's tail breaks off, it doesn't hurt. The bones in the gecko's tail have special cracks in them. The tail breaks off where the cracks are.

A TAIL WITH A MESSAGE The warthog has a tuft of fur at the end of its tail. When there is danger, the warthog holds its tail straight up in the air like a flag. Its high tail tells other warthogs to run away.

WATCH OUT! If you see a skunk's black-and-white tail up in the air, run! The skunk is afraid or angry. Skunks raise their tails before spraying their enemies with an awful-smelling scent.

HOLDING ON The opossum's long, skinny tail is just right for winding around things. It can even carry a pile of leaves that will make a soft bed for the opossum's babies.

TAILS ON ALERT Have you ever noticed how a squirrel sits up and flicks its tail back and forth? That means the squirrel has spotted danger.

IN THE LEAD Wolves use their long, fluffy tails to show who is the leader of the pack. The lead wolf often holds its tail higher than any of the other wolves do.

SWINGING TAILS A kangaroo's tail helps it travel fast and for a long time. The tail swings from side to side as the kangaroo hops. This swinging movement gives the kangaroo a little push as it bounces along.

Words to Know

balance An animal in balance can stand or move without tipping over.

flukes Flukes are a whale's flat tail fins.

hind legs Hind legs are back legs.

parasites Parasites are small animals or plants that can live on a larger animal's skin.

train A peacock's train is the male's tail feathers.

To Learn More

AT THE LIBRARY

Bodnar, Judit. *Tale of a Tail.* New York:
Lothrop, Lee & Shepard, 1998.

Fowler, Allan. *Telling Tails.* New York:
Children's Press, 1998.

Kawata, Ken. *Animal Tails.* Brooklyn, N.Y.:
Kane/Miller, 2001.

Swanson, Diane. *Tails That Talk and Fly.*
Vancouver: Greystone Books, 1999.

ON THE WEB

Lincoln Park Zoo

http://www.lpzoo.com

Explore the animals at the Lincoln Park Zoo.

San Diego Zoo

http://www.sandiegozoo.org

Learn about animals and their habitats.

Want to learn more about tails?

Visit FACT HOUND at

http://www.facthound.com

Index